JOHN COULTER

With French translations
by Raynald Desmeules

THE TRIAL
OF
LOUIS RIEL

PUBLISHED IN CANADA
BY OBERON PRESS

PRINTED AND BOUND IN ENGLAND
BY HAZELL WATSON AND VINEY LTD

For Douglas Lee

LOUIS RIEL

JUDGE: Mr. Justice Richardson

ASSOCIATE JUSTICE: Mr. Henry Le Jeune

CROWN: Christopher Robinson, Q.C., B. B. Osler, Q.C., G. W. Burbidge, Q.C., D. L. Scott (Mayor of Regina), T. C. Casgrain

DEFENCE: F. X. Lemieux, Charles Fitzpatrick, J. N. Greenshields, T. C. Johnston

WILLOUGHBY, MACKAY, NESS, KERR, JACKSON, MIDDLETON, NOLIN: Witnesses for the Crown

ANDRE, GARNOT, FOURMOND, ROY, CLARKE: Witnesses for the Defence

WALLACE, JUKES, PIGOTT: Crown witnesses in rebuttal

CLERK OF THE COURT

SHERIFF

MARCEAUX: Interpreter

FOREMAN OF THE JURY

Five JURYMEN

CONSTABLE

NORTH WEST MOUNTED POLICEMEN

REPORTERS

LAW STUDENTS

LIEUTENANT-GOVERNOR, MRS. RICHARDSON, MRS. MIDDLETON, MISS OSLER: Spectators

OFFICERS OF MILITIA

CITIZENS: Whites, Indians, half-breeds

As the members of the audience arrive at the courthouse they are scrutinized by a player costumed as a CONSTABLE *of the North West Mounted Police. On going in they see that the Court is not yet sitting. It is assembling.*

Various officials busy themselves with preparations. The CLERK OF THE COURT *sorts his papers.* REPORTERS *are taking their places, exchanging remarks.* LAW STUDENTS *prepare to take notes.*

Among the spectators are the LIEUTENANT-GOVERNOR, *officers of the militia and Mounties.* MRS. RICHARDSON (*wife of the* JUDGE), MRS. MIDDLETON (*wife of* GENERAL MIDDLETON, *who will testify*), MISS OSLER (*daughter of one of the counsel*). *Other ladies of social eminence. The gay colours of the ladies' hats and dresses and the scarlet uniforms of the officers lend the courtroom the aspect of a gala opening.*

Counsel arrive. They are dressed in pleated white shirts and white ties and they wear black gowns. No wigs. Counsel for the Crown dispose themselves at the end of the lawyers' table closest to the witness stand. Counsel for the Defence at the other end.

Witnesses arrive and take their seats. Six JURYMEN *come in and seat themselves below the bar.*

The CONSTABLE *comes in and whispers to the* CLERK, *then takes his place beside the* JURYMEN.

The CLERK *calls the Court to order.*

CLERK: Order! Order!

Everyone present, including the audience, rises and stands. The SHERIFF *enters. He is wearing a cocked hat, a frock coat or cutaway, with fichu and lace cuffs. He carries a sword with the blade resting on his shoulder. He halts and waits by the door while the* JUDGE (*Mr. Justice Richardson*) *and the* ASSOCIATE JUSTICE (*Mr. Henry Le Jeune*) *come in. They both wear black gowns. No wigs.*

The two justices take their place on the bench.

The SHERIFF *remains by the door.*

The JUDGE *bows to the lawyers.*

The lawyers return the bow and the Court is seated.

JUDGE: I have to announce that Mr. Henry Le Jeune will be Associate Justice with me for the approaching trial. The precept, please.

(CLERK *or* SHERIFF *hands the precept, which is a foolscap roll tied with ribbon.* JUDGE *removes the ribbon and tosses it aside. Then unrolls and glances through the precept—glances only. While the* JUDGE *is doing this the six* JURYMEN, *ushered into the courtroom by the* CONSTABLE, *take their places in the jurybox.*)

JUDGE (To CLERK): Poll the jury.

CLERK (To JURYMEN): When your name is called please stand up and say present. Francis Cosgrave.

COSGRAVE (*Rising*): Present. (*Sits again.*)

CONSTABLE: One.

CLERK: Harry J. Painter.

PAINTER: Present.

CONSTABLE: Two.

CLERK: Edwin J. Brooks.

BROOKS: Present.

CONSTABLE: Three.

CLERK: Walter Merryfield.

MERRYFIELD: Present.

CONSTABLE: Four.

CLERK: Edward Erratt.

ERRATT: Present.

CONSTABLE: Five.

CLERK: Peele Dean.

DEAN: Present. (*He remains standing.*)

CONSTABLE Six.

DEAN: Your Honour, I have some work I ought to be attending to. . . . I beg to be released.

JUDGE: I have no power to release you now, I am afraid. You were fairly drawn. (DEAN *sits down.*) Mr. Sheriff, will you bring in the prisoner? (SHERIFF *leaves to bring the prisoner. Counsel identify themselves.*)

CROWN (Christopher Robinson, Q.C.): I appear for the prosecution. With my learned friends, Mr. B. B. Osler, Q.C., Mr. G. W. Burbidge, Mr. Scott and Mr. Casgrain.

DEFENCE (F. X. Lemieux): I appear for the prisoner. With Mr. Charles Fitzpatrick, Mr. J. N. Greenshields and Mr. T. C. Johnston.

(SHERIFF *and* CONSTABLE *now bring in* RIEL, *who is shackled with ball and chain to his ankle. He carries the ball over his arm. He is in a black frock coat, white shirt and black cravat. He is bearded. Age, 41. He is placed in the dock. The* CONSTABLE *remains beside him. The* SHERIFF *goes to his place. He removes his hat and places it with his sword in front of him.*)

JUDGE: Louis Riel, have you been furnished with a copy of the charge, the panel of jurors and a list of witnesses for the prosecution?

RIEL: Yes, your Honour.

JUDGE: Arraign the prisoner.

CLERK (*Reading*): On this the 28th day of July in the year of our Lord 1885 at the town of Regina, Louis Riel you stand charged on oath that with divers other false traitors armed and arrayed in a warlike manner, you did levy and make war against our Lady the Queen, and did maliciously and traitorously attempt by force of arms to destroy the Constitution and Government of the Realm . . . and to depose our said Lady the Queen from the style and honour and kingly name of the Imperial Crown of the Realm to the evil example of others in like case offending. Louis Riel, are you guilty or not guilty?

RIEL: I have the honour to answer the Court I am not guilty.

CLERK: You may sit down. (RIEL *bows and sits.* JUDGE *nods to* CROWN, *who rises and addresses the Court.*)

CROWN (Osler): May it please your Honours, Gentlemen of the jury. The task before this Court is a momentous one. It is to pass judgment in what is probably the most serious trial ever to have taken place in Canada. To deal with it you must endeavour to bring to bear on the evidence, and on the evidence alone, your reason; and on that evidence you are to pronounce the prisoner guilty or innocent.

High treason, with which the prisoner stands charged, is the most serious offence known in this land. To bring it home to the prisoner we shall prove in evidence that he organized and led a rising in arms against the government.

For that purpose he returned in July 1884 from Montana to the Saskatchewan. In the months that followed he planned not only to force a change of government, but in its place to become himself the ruler of the country—or perish in the attempt.

When the time seemed ripe to make the attempt, he stated in the presence of witnesses that in one week the government police would be wiped out of existence. He wrote and signed a document in which he stated (*picks up and reads a paper*), "We intend to commence a war of extermination upon all who have shown themselves hostile to our rights." A few days later he told another witness that the rebellion had started. That he had been waiting fifteen years to start it.

On March 18 he sent out a large body of men who busied themselves looting and taking prisoners. Looting stores at or near Batoche.

On this, the authorities became alarmed. Still, Major Crozier, superintendent of the North West Mounted Police in the area, did what he could to allay passion, to avert trouble. He tried to persuade those poor deluded men, incited and inflamed by the prisoner, to lay aside their arms and go home in peace. The prisoner's reply was an insolent demand for the unconditional surrender of Fort Carlton, headquarters there of Crozier and his forces.

There could be but one response. Fighting followed. First at Duck Lake. We find a letter from Riel to the half-breeds at Qu'Appelle telling of victory at Duck Lake. And other similar letters: to the half-breeds at Battleford; to the Indians—"dear relatives"—asking for aid. Showing the need of overturning the government. Urging the Indians to rise.

A letter found in the camp of the Indian chieftain Poundmaker proves the deliberate intention of the prisoner to bring upon the country the calamity of an Indian war. That war was, in fact, already joined. Riel had already won what he thought was a decisive victory. There is a document in his hand inviting the authorities to come and take away their dead from the field of battle. For this they had his gracious permission.

Three days later the scene of the fight had shifted. To Fish Creek, with the police and militia now under the command of General Middleton. In ten days time the struggle had moved to Batoche, where it continued for yet another four days when it was finally stamped out. Stamped out at loss of much suffering and misery and sacrifice of men's lives.

Responsibility for this—for initiating and continuing this struggle, for giving the order to fire on the police and militia—responsibility for this we will bring home to that man in the dock. That is the act of war with which he stands charged.

We shall further bring home to him that in this treasonable and dastardly undertaking, he acted not so much for the well-being of the half-breeds whom he led as for his own enrichment. We will show that he was prepared—at a price, for a sum of money in the form of an indemnity to be paid him by the government—he was prepared to end the rebellion and leave the country. (*Pauses.*)

Now as to the means by which Riel accomplished this —the means by which he was able to raise and lead this rebellion, the means by which he acquired and retained his power over his followers. He was shrewd, full of cunning, ruthless, unscrupulous and of superior education. To attain his ends there was no length to which he would not go. Instance his tactic when he found the Church to which he belonged, and to which his principal supporters belonged, was against him. His answer was to pose as a prophet. Prophet of a new religion. Prophet of the Saskatchewan. Of the New World. That was the cry under which his dupes were rallied. Under which the wrongs of the half-breeds were to be put to rights.

I think, Gentlemen of the Jury, I think you will be satisfied before this case is over, that the rebellion was not brought about by the wrongs of the half-breeds so much as by the personal ambition and vanity of that man on trial.

We seek to bring home to him the crime of treason. Treason involving the shedding of brave men's blood. Treason which roused the whole country. Treason crying out from the dead bodies lying on the blood-stained snow. Treason which brought an answering response from end to end of the land—an armed force from the east, from every town and city and hamlet men rallying to protect their fellow-men and the integrity of their country. (*Pauses impressively.*) Let all take note of this, and tremble at the power to punish invoked by such a crime.

Now, Gentlemen of the Jury, it will be for you to consider carefully the evidence we shall put before you, and then to say whether the Crown has made out its case, and whether there be any real doubt of the prisoner's guilt.

CROWN (Robinson): We wish to call in evidence Dr. John Willoughby. (WILLOUGHBY *takes witness stand and is sworn by* CONSTABLE.) Dr. Willoughby, you are a medical man?

WILLOUGHBY: Yes.

CROWN: Where are you practising?

WILLOUGHBY: At Saskatoon.

CROWN: Since when?

WILLOUGHBY: Two years last May.

CROWN: How far is Saskatoon from Batoche?

WILLOUGHBY: About fifty miles.

CROWN: Do you remember going to Batoche the 16th of March last?

WILLOUGHBY: I do.

CROWN: When you reached Batoche what did you do?

WILLOUGHBY: I went to Kerr's store.

CROWN: While there did you hear anything of possible trouble brewing?

WILLOUGHBY: I did hear rumours, but I left almost at once with a Mr. Welsh who was on his way to find Riel. We found him at the house of a half-breed called Rocheleau.

CROWN: At that time did you know Riel?

WILLOUGHBY: I knew him by sight. And I had met and spoken to him before.

CROWN: What happened? What was said, when you found him at Rocheleau's?

WILLOUGHBY: He said the time had come for the half-breeds to assert their rights. He walked up and down in front of me. Suddenly he stopped and turned to me and said, "The time has come when it would be better for a man to have lived a good life."

CROWN: What did you understand him to mean by that?

WILLOUGHBY: That some of us would not be living much longer.

CROWN: Did you reply?

WILLOUGHBY: I said it would be better for a man always to live a good life and be ready for anything.

CROWN: What happened next?

WILLOUGHBY: A large crowd of men drove up to the door.

CROWN: How many would you say?

WILLOUGHBY: About sixty or seventy.

CROWN: Were they half-breeds?

WILLOUGHBY: Half-breeds.

CROWN: Armed?

WILLOUGHBY: Armed.

CROWN: All of them armed?

WILLOUGHBY: I only saw one who wasn't armed.

CROWN: What were they armed with?

WILLOUGHBY: Shotguns.

CROWN: Did the prisoner say anything about these armed men?

WILLOUGHBY: He said he and they intended to strike a blow for their rights.

CROWN: Did you reply?

WILLOUGHBY: Yes. I said there were different ways of getting your rights. I said the white settlers took a different way. That nettled him. He snapped back that nobody knew better than he did about the white settlers and their grievances. He said he had petitioned the government for them over and over again. But no answer. No answer but police. Always police. More police.

CROWN: What did he say next?

WILLOUGHBY: He said, "But that's over now." He pointed to those men outside and said, "Now I have my own police. In one week they will have wiped out the government police."

CROWN: Wiped them out?

WILLOUGHBY: "Wiped them out of existence," that's what he said.

CROWN: Go on.

WILLOUGHBY: I said if he raised a rebellion and attacked the police the white settlers should be protected because they had nothing against the half-breeds.

CROWN: Then?

WILLOUGHBY: He said as I was from Saskatoon I had no right to be asking protection.

CROWN: Did he say why?

WILLOUGHBY: He said because last fall the people of Saskatoon took the part of the mounted police at Battleford. Offered to help them kill the Indians and half-breeds. "Now," he said. "Now we will show Saskatoon who will do the killing."

CROWN: Go on.

WILLOUGHBY: He said as soon as he struck the first blow here he would have help. From across the border. The United States would be behind him.

CROWN: The United States?

WILLOUGHBY: He said he was an American citizen from Montana. He said the half-breeds here had called him to come across the border and help them. He said they had plans but he told them their plans were no good. *He* had plans. Plans that would bring results. Practical results. Then he looked at me and added, "You know me. You know my history. So you will know I mean what I say. And I say the time has come for me to take charge here. To rule this country. And I *will* rule it—or perish in the attempt."

CROWN: Can you tell us more?

WILLOUGHBY: He told me he would set up a government of God-fearing men—not like the men in the government at Ottawa. They would then divide the country into seven portions and these would be allotted to immigrants of various nationalities: the Germans, the Irish, the Italians and so on. He said there would be a new Ireland in the Northwest. (*Laughter in court. Suppressed.*)

CROWN: Did he make any reference to the rebellion he led at Red River fifteen years ago?

WILLOUGHBY: Yes. He said it wouldn't be a patch on the rebellion he was starting now. This time a lot more would be killed.

CROWN: What happened after that?

WILLOUGHBY: He went out and dismissed his half-breeds. Sent them to Champagne's house, I think. Most of them drove away.

CROWN: And then?

WILLOUGHBY: Then we had dinner.

CROWN (*Affecting astonishment*): Dinner?

WILLOUGHBY: Yes.

CROWN: Oh!

WILLOUGHBY: Oh yes. And I must say prisoner made himself most agreeable. When he was leaving he was specially polite.

CROWN: He left first?

WILLOUGHBY: Yes. As he left he asked me to believe he had no ill-feelings towards me personally. He said it was only that I was a Canadian. Therefore I was for the Canadian government, so we could have no real friendship in our hearts toward each other.

CROWN: After he left what did you do?

WILLOUGHBY: I started immediately for Clark's Crossing —the telegraph office.

CROWN: For what purpose?

WILLOUGHBY: To get in touch with Regina and let them know what was happening.

CROWN: Did you get in touch with Regina?

WILLOUGHBY: No.

CROWN: Why?

WILLOUGHBY: The wires were down.

CROWN: What did you do?

WILLOUGHBY: The only communication was with Battleford. I got Colonel Morris there and told him.

CROWN: Who is Colonel Morris?

WILLOUGHBY: He was in charge of the police at Battleford at the time.

CROWN: You told him all that had passed?

WILLOUGHBY: I did.

CROWN: Well now, have you told me all you remember? Of your talk with Riel?

WILLOUGHBY: I remember one other point raised by Riel. It was about Orangemen.

CROWN: What was that?

WILLOUGHBY: He said they would have no Orangemen in the Northwest. I said I hoped by Orangemen he didn't mean Protestants. At that he wheeled round excitedly and said he certainly understood the difference between Orangemen and Protestants. Then he went on about the different religions and beliefs and said they were all part of one tree. Branches of one tree. He said the biggest branch was at the bottom and that was the true Church. His Church, of course. The Roman Catholic Church.

CROWN: Now have you told us all you remember of what the prisoner said?

WILLOUGHBY: I believe I have.

CROWN: Thank you. (CROWN *gives place to* DEFENCE.)

DEFENCE (Fitzpatrick): In the interview you have described with the prisoner, was he armed?

WILLOUGHBY: Not then. Not that I could see.

DEFENCE: You said he spoke of plans for giving portions of the Northwest to people of various nationalities. Did he say why this would be done?

WILLOUGHBY: Yes. He said these people would help in the rebellion and they would have their reward.

DEFENCE: Did he explain what negotiations, if any, he had made to be sure of help from these people?

WILLOUGHBY: He did not.

DEFENCE: Did you ask him?

WILLOUGHBY: No.

DEFENCE: Don't you think it would have been a very necessary question? Or did you think such ideas, such plans, entirely reasonable?

WILLOUGHBY: I had my own opinion about them.

DEFENCE: What was it?

WILLOUGHBY: That nothing more would be heard of them.

DEFENCE: All that talk of dividing up the Northwest and giving it away in this fashion—did it strike you as in any way peculiar or extraordinary?

WILLOUGHBY: It did, of course. I thought it simply nonsensical.

DEFENCE: Not rational? Not sane?

WILLOUGHBY: That's right.

DEFENCE: Thank you. (DEFENCE *gives place to* CROWN *for re-examination.*)

CROWN (Robinson): You said Riel wasn't armed during the interview described?

WILLOUGHBY: Not in the house. But as he got into the sleigh to drive off after dinner, he was given a gun.

CROWN: By whom?

WILLOUGHBY: I don't know.

CROWN: Thank you. That is all. (WILLOUGHBY *goes back to his place among the other witnesses.*)

CROWN (Robinson): Mr. Thomas Mackay. (MACKAY *comes to the witness box and is sworn.*) Where do you live, Mr. Mackay?

MACKAY: Prince Albert.

CROWN: You were born in this country?

MACKAY: Yes.

CROWN: Do you remember the disturbances last March?

MACKAY: I do.

CROWN: Tell us what you remember.

MACKAY: I was one of forty men in Prince Albert who answered a call from Major Crozier. A call for volunteers. We marched all day. Forty miles. To Fort Carlton.

CROWN: What happened when you got there?

MACKAY: We found a letter had arrived calling on Major Crozier to surrender Fort Carlton.

CROWN: A letter from whom?

MACKAY: The prisoner. Because of the letter I left for

Riel · 15

Batoche, where the prisoner and his half-breeds had their headquarters.

CROWN: What did you go there for?

MACKAY: To warn them of the danger they were getting into and try to persuade them not to go on with the rising.

CROWN: When you reached Batoche did you meet the prisoner?

MACKAY: I did.

CROWN: How were you received?

MACKAY: The prisoner called me a traitor. A traitor to *his* government. He said except for traitors like me—white settlers—the half-breed's grievances would have been put to rights long ago. He said now he was out to end all that. Out for blood—and the first blood he wanted, he said, was mine. He picked up a spoon from the table and put it close to my face, and said all the little blood I had in me would be there in five minutes. He wanted to put me on trial for my life for helping the authorities. But he had a committee meeting upstairs. He had to go to it. He came down later and apologized to me for the way he had spoken to me. He said he wished I was with *them*. But he warned me there would be bloodshed if Crozier didn't surrender Fort Carlton. After that I left.

CROWN: Where did you go?

MACKAY: Back to Fort Carlton.

CROWN: And when you got there?

MACKAY: I found that Crozier had rejected Riel's demand for surrender. Later there was fighting. Ten of our men were left on the field. One of them made his way in afterwards, badly wounded.

CROWN: And the other nine?

MACKAY: They were dead.

CROWN: How many were killed on the other side?

MACKAY: I don't know.

CROWN: What happened after that?

MACKAY: Fort Carlton was evacuated. We retired to Prince Albert.

CROWN: You yourself went back there?

MACKAY: Yes, and stayed there during the rest of the rebellion. (CROWN *gives place to* DEFENCE.)

DEFENCE (Greenshields): You mentioned Riel's desire to have the half-breeds' grievances put right. What grievances?

MACKAY: They were entitled to scrip for their lands and the government never gave it. Riel said they had been trying for fifteen years to get it with no result. He didn't need to tell me. I knew all about it. It was the same for the white settlers. I said that to Riel, and he said now they would do something about it.

DEFENCE: You mentioned that the prisoner picked up a spoon from the table. What else, if anything, was on that table?

MACKAY: Some tin dishes and other spoons. Some fried bacon and some bannocks.

DEFENCE: Any blood in the dishes—cooked blood?

MACKAY: Not that I saw.

DEFENCE: Was the prisoner in a very excited state when he talked about blood?

MACKAY: He became very excited.

DEFENCE: In what position was he at the time?

MACKAY: Standing there striking the table.

DEFENCE: And saying he would have your blood in that spoon?

MACKAY: That's right.

DEFENCE: You say he wanted to put you on trial for your life. Did he try to make you prisoner or were you at perfect liberty to go?

MACKAY: I was at liberty to go.

DEFENCE: On the whole he treated you civilly?

MACKAY: No, he did not. He used language to me that was never used to me before.

DEFENCE: But he apologized for it later?

MACKAY: Oh yes.

DEFENCE: And was polite?

MACKAY: Sure. All over himself being polite.

DEFENCE: Did all this behaviour strike you as being quite normal?

MACKAY: I thought it was just crazy.

DEFENCE: Thank you. (DEFENCE *retires but* MACKAY *remains on the stand.*)

JUDGE: Any juror who wishes to ask any question of the witness is at liberty to do so.

(*Pause of six seconds. No questions.* JUDGE *nods his permission to witness to go. He goes.*)

CROWN (Burbidge): I wish to call Mr. James Ness. (NESS *takes the stand and is sworn.*) You are a farmer?

NESS: Yes.

CROWN: And a Justice of the Peace?

NESS: I am.

CROWN: Where do you live?

NESS: Near Batoche.

CROWN: Have you seen and talked to Riel there?

NESS: Several times.

CROWN: You knew of his movements?

NESS: Yes.

CROWN: Did he attend church regularly?

NESS: Yes.

CROWN: Do you know if he was on good terms with the priests?

NESS: One day in front of the church Riel started saying he was a prophet. And that he could foretell events. Father

Moulin protested and Riel shouted, "Look at him! He is a Protestant! We will take him prisoner. We will lock him up. Tie him up." Then Riel went in and took possession of the church.

CROWN: What for?

NESS: To lock up his prisoners.

CROWN: Did he take you prisoner?

NESS: Yes.

CROWN: Why?

NESS: I was against him. For the authorities.

CROWN: Did he punish you?

NESS: He took my horse and my cutter and robe.

CROWN: And then let you go?

NESS: Only after I gave a solemn promise to be neutral.

CROWN: Why did you promise to be neutral?

NESS: I have a wife and family. When I got home that night my wife was in a terrible state. Some Sioux Indians had told her I was shot. She thought I was shot.

CROWN: Had you been in danger of being shot?

NESS: I thought so. We were all living in a state of terror.

CROWN: Because of what?

NESS: Because Riel was bent on making trouble. A hot-head with a lighted match and a keg of gunpowder. (CROWN *gives place to* DEFENCE.)

DEFENCE (Fitzpatrick): You saw Riel take possession of the church?

NESS: Yes.

DEFENCE: Did you yourself hear what he said to Father Moulin?

NESS: I did.

DEFENCE: Up to that time had you ever heard him make any derogatory remarks about the priests?

NESS: I heard him accusing Bishop Taché and Bishop Grandin of being thieves and rogues.

DEFENCE: Did he make a general onslaught on all parties connected with the Roman Catholic Church?

NESS: Yes.

DEFENCE: Now, can you recall anything more of what he said to Father Moulin that day outside the church? Or of what Father Moulin said to him?

NESS: Riel said the Spirit of God was in him, Riel. And Father Moulin denounced him and said he was making a schism within the Church. But Riel replied that Rome had fallen.

DEFENCE: Proceed, please.

NESS: He said the Pope of Rome was not legally Pope.

DEFENCE: He said the episcopate spirit had left Rome and come into the Northwest?

NESS: No, he did not say that.

DEFENCE: But he did say something of that kind?

NESS: He said the Spirit of God was in him, Riel. And that Rome had fallen. And that he was a prophet and could foretell events.

DEFENCE: Yet he attended church as Roman Catholics generally do?

NESS: Yes. He was very pious. Very devout.

DEFENCE: Very devout. Yet at the same time saying such things and threatening the priests. How did such conduct strike you?

NESS: Well, I thought he was a bit touched in the head.

DEFENCE: Thank you. (DEFENCE *gives place to* CROWN. NESS *returns to his seat among the witnesses.*)

CROWN (Casgrain): Mr George Kerr. (KERR *takes the stand and is sworn.*) Mr. Kerr, you keep a store at Batoche?

KERR: Yes. With my brother. We are partners.

CROWN: On March 18th did the prisoner come to your store?

KERR: He did. With Gabriel Dumont and about fifty other half-breeds and Indians.

CROWN: Were they armed?

KERR: They were all armed.

CROWN: What did they do at the store on that occasion?

KERR: They demanded guns and ammunition.

CROWN: What did you say?

KERR: I told them they were up on the shelf. The store has cross-beams and the guns were on the cross-beams. The half-breeds came around to take them. Round behind the counter. But Riel stopped them and said, "Who is boss here?" I said I was. And he said, "They have no right to go behind your counter. But give them what they want and charge it."

CROWN: Did you give them what they wanted?

KERR: They took it.

CROWN: How much ammunition did they take from your store?

KERR: A keg of powder and six English double-barrel guns.

CROWN: Anything else?

KERR: Yes. A box of Ballard rifle cartridges.

CROWN: You say Riel asked you to charge these things?

KERR: He said I was to keep account and I would be paid.

CROWN: Were you paid?

KERR: No.

CROWN: Did you present the account?

KERR: How could I? He was a prisoner before I could.

CROWN: Meantime were you able to carry on your usual business in the store?

KERR: No. There was nothing left to carry on with. You see, the store was looted. Cleaned right out.

CROWN: By whom?

KERR: Half-breeds and Indians. They broke into the store and cleaned everything right out.

CROWN: Where were you at the time they broke in?

KERR: My brother and I were at Mrs. Venn's, where we were stopping. On our way back to the store we met a load of half-breed women and Indians with packs on their backs—frying pans and things. I said to my brother, "Jack," I said. "Jack, these things are ours." I asked one of the women and she said, "Yes, sure. We took them." When we got to the store there were four or five Indians pulling nails out of the beams. They left nothing. The store was upside down. The Fairbanks scale upside down. Nothing was left in the store at all.

CROWN: Can you tell us anything else that took place at your store?

KERR: Riel and his Council met there.

CROWN: For what purpose?

KERR: They were trying prisoners and making plans.

CROWN: Prisoners?

KERR: Anyone who was against them or making trouble for them.

CROWN: And what plans?

KERR: I believe they were making plans to destroy the police and then set up a government of their own instead.

CROWN: Do you know this of your own knowledge?

KERR: Everybody knew it. There wasn't any doubt about it. Riel was boasting about it. I heard him.

CROWN: What did you hear him say?

KERR: That he would wipe the police out of existence before they knew what was up.

CROWN: At that time what was the general state of the country?

KERR: The whole country was excited, very excited. Everybody rushing about wondering what next and asking what would happen.

CROWN: Did you see people under arms?

KERR: Yes. All over the place. Everywhere they were under arms. (CROWN *gives place to* DEFENCE.)

DEFENCE (Fitzpatrick): You spoke of meetings at your store. Did you attend any meeting at which Riel was present?

KERR: Yes.

DEFENCE: When was that?

KERR: In January, I think.

DEFENCE: Can you remember what took place at that meeting?

KERR: Some money was presented to Riel.

DEFENCE: What money? Where did it come from?

KERR: The people had gathered it. I gave a dollar myself.

DEFENCE: Can you tell us more about the meeting?

KERR: My brother and I were invited. There was a supper. The prisoner was there. I guess there were 150 people there. It was a pretty good spread. Riel made my brother and me sit at the head table. At the end of the head table.

DEFENCE: Were speeches made?

KERR: Lots of speeches.

DEFENCE: Did Riel speak?

KERR: Oh yes.

DEFENCE: What did he say?

KERR: I don't rightly remember all he said. There was an awful lot of it. But some of it was about us all being loyal subjects of Her Majesty. He said we would all still be loyal subjects if the right thing was done by us. He proposed the Queen's health. I remember the words. "The health of our Sovereign Queen Victoria!"

DEFENCE: The health of our Sovereign Queen Victoria?

KERR: Yes.

DEFENCE: Riel said that? Proposed that toast?

KERR: He did.

DEFENCE: Was any treason talked?

Riel · 23

KERR: Not that I heard. Not a word.

DEFENCE: Those 150 were all present together as loyal subjects toasting the Queen?

KERR: Yes.

DEFENCE: That was in January. Two months before the prisoner decided there was nothing for it but to resort to arms?

KERR: That's right.

DEFENCE: Thank you, Mr. Kerr.

KERR: Thank you, sir. (DEFENCE *gives place to* CROWN.)

CROWN (Osler): Mr. Thomas E. Jackson. (KERR *returns to his place and* JACKSON *enters the stand and is sworn.*) You live at Prince Albert, Mr. Jackson?

JACKSON: I do.

CROWN: You are a druggist?

JACKSON: I am.

CROWN: Had you occasion to go to Duck Lake at the time of the fighting there?

JACKSON: Yes.

CROWN: Did you see the prisoner there?

JACKSON: I did. I talked to him.

CROWN: What passed between you?

JACKSON: He spoke about having had to take up arms. He said he had no wish to molest the white settlers. He said his quarrel was with the government and the police and the Hudson's Bay Company. He said he gave orders to fire only when Major Crozier fired first.

CROWN: He gave orders to fire?

JACKSON: Yes, he said so. He told me that after Crozier's first volley he said to his men, "In the name of God the Father who created us, reply to that." Then after the second volley from Crozier, "In the name of God the Son who saved us, reply to that." And after the third volley, "In the name of God the Holy Ghost who sanctifies us, reply to that." He said he repeated his commands in that fashion all through the battle.

CROWN: Thank you. (CROWN *gives place to* DEFENCE.)

DEFENCE: Did the language used by Riel in giving orders strike you as at all . . . peculiar?

JACKSON: It was certainly very unusual.

DEFENCE: He seems to have been a very religious man?

JACKSON: Everything seemed to be religion with him. He had his own ideas about religion.

DEFENCE: Did you know of his idea that the Pope was not legally Pope?

JACKSON: I did.

DEFENCE: How did you know?

JACKSON: I heard him say it himself. I heard him say, too, that the Pope was in his way. That there had to be a new Pope. Someone from this country.

DEFENCE: Did he ever mention in your hearing who in this country should take the place of the Pope?

JACKSON: I think himself.

DEFENCE: You heard him say this?

JACKSON: No. But it was pretty clear he intended to take the position himself.

DEFENCE: Did it seem to you a reasonable idea that Riel should think of making himself Pope?

JACKSON: I thought it sort of—funny.

DEFENCE: Funny?

JACKSON: Well, it was that daft.

DEFENCE: Thank you. (JACKSON *joins the other witnesses.* CROWN *replaces* DEFENCE.)

CROWN (Robinson): General Frederick Middleton. (MIDDLETON *takes the stand and is sworn. He is in uniform.*) You are a Major-General in Her Majesty's service?

MIDDLETON: Yes.

CROWN: What position do you hold in Canada?

MIDDLETON: I am in command of the home militia force.

CROWN: Were you called in for service in the Territories?

MIDDLETON: Yes. On the 23rd of March. I started immediately.

CROWN: When did you reach Batoche?

MIDDLETON: On the morning of the 9th of May.

CROWN: You engaged the rebel forces?

MIDDLETON: Yes. The moment I got there.

CROWN: The engagement continued until . . .?

MIDDLETON: The 12th. When Batoche was taken.

CROWN: How long after that until the prisoner was brought to you?

MIDDLETON: I think it was on the 15th. I had sent out all the scouts to scour the woods as far as Batoche. On the 15th Riel was brought in by two scouts, Hourie and Armstrong. Brought to my tent. As Riel entered he produced a paper which I had sent to him. In it I had said if he surrendered I would protect him until his case was decided by the Canadian Government.

CROWN: What was done with him then?

MIDDLETON: I kept him in my tent all day. Few knew he was there. Then I had a tent pitched beside mine. I put him in there under charge of Captain Young and two sentries with loaded arms. Captain Young slept in the tent with the prisoner.

CROWN: And after that?

MIDDLETON: I telegraphed down to the government to say Mr. Riel was my prisoner and what should I do with him? I was directed to send him to Regina, which I did, under charge of Captain Young with twelve men and a sergeant. (CROWN *gives place to* DEFENCE.)

DEFENCE (Greenshields): During the time Riel was in your tent, did you talk to him about his religious views?

MIDDLETON: Well, yes. Or rather he talked to me. Never

stopped talking. I remember thinking, "Confound him, he's always bothering about his religion. He's anxious you should know about his religion."

DEFENCE: Did his talk seem to you the talk of a well-balanced individual?

MIDDLETON: I thought it just the talk of a religious enthusiast. He seemed to me a man imbued with a strong, morbid religious feeling mingled with intense personal vanity.

DEFENCE: You spoke of a letter brought you by the prisoner when he came to your tent. A letter you had sent him.

MIDDLETON: Yes.

DEFENCE (*Handing the letter*): Is that the letter?

MIDDLETON (*Looking at it*): Yes, that is the same.

DEFENCE: Exhibit I. What were the circumstances under which you had sent that letter?

MIDDLETON: It was my reply to one from Riel. I had gone off with the cavalry and guns to the right—a feint, to draw the enemy from our left, to make as much show as possible and keep the enemy engaged. It was an engagement at quite long bowls. In the middle of it a man, a Mr. Astley, came galloping up with a white flag. He waved a letter—the one from Riel. He tried to tell me something but I couldn't hear. The noise of the guns was too great. But in a lull I understood him to say that Mr. Riel was in a very great state of excitement and might be ready to surrender. That's what was in the letter. I scribbled my answer on the back of the envelope. There it is. That's the letter Mr. Riel brought to my tent.

DEFENCE: When Astley said the prisoner was perhaps ready to surrender, did he mention as a condition of surrender that Riel wished to be recognized as head of the new Church he had formed at Batoche?

MIDDLETON: I don't think so. If he had—if he had proposed anything so idiotic—I fear I should have used some pretty strong language.

DEFENCE: You would have refused a request so—so idiotic?

MIDDLETON: Certainly, sir. And seized the messenger.

DEFENCE (*Pointedly weighing it*): Idiotic.

MIDDLETON: What?

DEFENCE (*With covert satisfaction*): Thank you, General. (MIDDLETON, *suspicious and a little resentful, retires.* DEFENCE *gives place to* CROWN.)

CROWN (Casgrain): Mr. Charles Nolin. (NOLIN *is sworn.*) As the witness has some difficulty with English. . . .

JUDGE: We shall hear his evidence through an interpreter. Mr. Marceaux. (MARCEAUX *bows to the court and takes his place beside the witness.*)

CROWN: You know the prisoner?

MARCEAUX: Vous connaissez le prisonnier?

NOLIN: C'est mon cousin.

MARCEAUX: He is my cousin.

CROWN: You met him during the insurrection?

MARCEAUX: Vous l'avez rencontré au cours de l'insurrection?

NOLIN: Maintes fois. A son arrivée du Montana, il a demeuré avec moi dans ma maison.

MARCEAUX: Many times. When he came here from Montana he stayed with me in my house.

CROWN: Did he do or say anything to acquaint you with his plans?

MARCEAUX: A-t-il fait ou dit quoi que ce soit pour vous mettre au courant de ses desseins?

NOLIN: Il m'a montré un livre qu'il avait écrit aux États. Il y racontait qu'il allait détruire l'Angleterre et le Canada. La ville de Rome, aussi, et le pape.

MARCEAUX: He showed me a book he had written in the States. In it he said he would destroy England and Canada. Also Rome and the Pope.

(*During the examination of this witness* RIEL *is specially alert and attentive. He takes copious notes. He grows more and more impatient. In what follows he will seem at moments about to jump up and intervene, but restrains himself. There is obvious distrust and hostility between him and the witness.*)

CROWN: When he talked to you, what did he talk about?

MARCEAUX: Quand il vous parlait, de quoi vous parlait-il?

NOLIN: Entre autres choses, d'argent. Il disait qu'il voulait obtenir une indemnité du gouvernement canadien, qui lui devait $100,000.

MARCEAUX: For one thing, money. He said he wanted an indemnity from the Canadian government, which owed him $100,000.

CROWN: Owed what for?

MARCEAUX: Pourquoi le gouvernement lui devait-il cet argent?

NOLIN: Pour la perte de sa propriété. Quand ils l'ont expulsé du Manitoba il y a quinze ans. Et parce qu'il a dû vivre en exil durant ces quinze années. Il me disait que le père André l'aidait à obtenir l'argent.

MARCEAUX: Loss of property. When they drove him out of Manitoba fifteen years ago. And for having been forced to live in exile those fifteen years. He told me Father André was helping him to get the money.

CROWN: But was he not at war with the priests?

MARCEAUX: Mais n'était-il pas en guerre contre les prêtres?

NOLIN: Il disait qu'il avait signé la paix avec eux. . . .

MARCEAUX: He said he had made his peace with the priests. . . .

NOLIN: Il disait qu'il était allé à l'église avec le père André. . . .

MARCEAUX: He said he went to the church with Father André. . . .

NOLIN: Et qu'en présence d'un autre prêtre et du Saint-Sacrement. . . .

MARCEAUX: And in the presence of another priest and the Blessed Sacrament. . . .

NOLIN: Il avait promis de ne plus jamais rien faire contre le clergé. . . .

MARCEAUX: He promised never again to do anything against the clergy. . . .

NOLIN: C'est pour cette raison que le père André était d'accord pour user de son influence auprès du gouvernement. Pour tâcher d'obtenir à Riel $35,000.

MARCEAUX: For that Father André was to use his influence with the government. To try to get Riel $35,000.

CROWN: Thirty-five thousand? Not a hundred thousand?

MARCEAUX: Trente-cinq mille? Pourquoi pas cent mille?

NOLIN: Riel disait qu'il prendrait trente-cinq mille tout de suite et qu'il s'arrangerait lui-même pour obtenir du gouvernement le reste des cent mille.

MARCEAUX: Riel said he would take thirty-five thousand now and get the rest of the hundred thousand out of the government himself.

CROWN: Did he say what he proposed to do if he got the money?

MARCEAUX: A-t-il dit ce qu'il avait l'intention de faire s'il obtenait l'argent?

NOLIN: Il disait qu'il mettrait fin à la rébellion et qu'il s'en irait où le gouvernement voudrait. . . .

MARCEAUX: He said he would stop the rebellion and go wherever the government wanted him to go. . . .

NOLIN: Mais il disait aussi qu'il irait aux États-Unis et qu'il fonderait un journal.

MARCEAUX: But he also said he would go to the United States and start a newspaper.

CROWN: Had he any particular object in view in starting a newspaper?

MARCEAUX: Avait-il un but précis pour fonder un journal?

NOLIN: Il disait qu'il s'en servirait pour forcer le gouvernement à rendre justice aux métis. . . .

MARCEAUX: He said he would use it to force the government to do right by the half-breeds. . . .

NOLIN: Il disait que l'Angleterre avait volé les métis pendant 400 ans, mais qu'il allait mettre fin à ça.

MARCEAUX: He said England had robbed the half-breeds for 400 years, but now he would put a stop to that.

CROWN: What happened about the $35,000?

MARCEAUX: Qu'est-il advenu des $35,000?

NOLIN: J'ai reçu un télégramme du premier ministre Macdonald d'Ottawa. Il promettait réparation pour les métis. De la demande de Riel, pas un mot.

MARCEAUX: I received a telegram from Prime Minister Macdonald in Ottawa. It promised redress for the half-breeds. But of Riel's claim, not a word.

CROWN: Did Riel see that telegram?

MARCEAUX: Est-ce que Riel a vu ce télégramme?

NOLIN: Je le lui ai montré.

MARCEAUX: I showed it to him.

CROWN: What did he say?

MARCEAUX: Qu'est-ce qu'il a dit?

NOLIN: Il a dit: "Avant que l'herbe soit haute comme ça, vous allez voir des armées étrangères dans ce pays."

MARCEAUX: He said, "Before the grass is that high, you will see foreign armies in this country."

CROWN: Were you present at an interview between Riel

and Father André about the setting up of a provisional government?

MARCEAUX: Étiez-vous présent à un entretien entre Riel et le père André au sujet de l'établissement d'un gouvernement provisoire?

NOLIN: Oui.

MARCEAUX: Yes.

CROWN: What happened?

MARCEAUX: Que s'est-il passé?

NOLIN: Riel exigeait que le père André lui donne la permission de proclamer le gouvernement provisoire avant minuit ce soir-là.

MARCEAUX: Riel demanded that Father André give him permission to proclaim a provisional government before twelve o'clock that night.

CROWN: When was that? What date?

MARCEAUX: Quand était-ce? Quelle date?

NOLIN: Le deux mars.

MARCEAUX: The 2nd of March.

CROWN: What happened?

MARCEAUX: Que s'est-il passé ensuite?

NOLIN: Le père André a refusé de donner sa permission.

MARCEAUX: Father André refused to give him permission.

CROWN: So?

MARCEAUX: Alors?

NOLIN: Ils se sont disputés. Ils étaient tous les deux très en colère. Surtout Riel. Le père André l'a mis à la porte.

MARCEAUX: They had a row. They were very angry. Especially Riel. Father André put him out the door.

CROWN: After that?

MARCEAUX: Et après ça?

NOLIN: J'ai rompu avec Riel.

MARCEAUX: I broke with Riel.

CROWN: And . . .?

MARCEAUX: Et . . .?

NOLIN: J'ai été fait prisonnier. Traduit en justice. Condamné à mort, mais je me suis évadé.

MARCEAUX: I was taken prisoner and tried. I was condemned to death, but I escaped.

CROWN: Why had you joined Riel in the first place?

MARCEAUX: Pourquoi vous étiez-vous joint à Riel au tout début?

NOLIN: Il le fallait. Pour avoir la vie sauve.

MARCEAUX: I had to. To save my life. (CROWN *gives place to* DEFENCE.)

DEFENCE (Lemieux): You said the prisoner came to your house from Montana. What was he doing in Montana?

MARCEAUX: Vous avez dit que le prisonnier était allé chez vous en arrivant du Montana. Que faisait-il au Montana?

NOLIN: Il y vivait avec sa femme et ses enfants. Il enseignait à l'école.

MARCEAUX: Living there with his wife and children. Teaching school.

DEFENCE: Why did he come from Montana?

MARCEAUX: Pourquoi est-il parti du Montana?

NOLIN: On avait envoyé une députation lui demander de prêter main-forte.

MARCEAUX: A deputation was sent to ask him to come and help.

DEFENCE: Help whom?

MARCEAUX: A qui?

NOLIN: Aux métis et aux colons blancs.

MARCEAUX: The half-breeds and white settlers.

DEFENCE: Help with what?

MARCEAUX: Pourquoi?

NOLIN: Pour forcer le gouvernement à reconnaître la propriété de leurs terres.

MARCEAUX: With getting scrip for their lands from the government.

DEFENCE: Did the clergy take part in the movement?

MARCEAUX: Est-ce que le clergé a pris part à cette affaire?

NOLIN: Oui. Le clergé de toutes les sectes et de toutes les religions.

MARCEAUX: Yes. The clergy of all denominations.

DEFENCE: Did the prisoner ever tell you he considered himself a prophet?

MARCEAUX: Le prisonnier vous a-t-il jamais dit qu'il se considérait comme un prophète?

NOLIN: Oui, il me l'a dit. Un soir, son ventre fit un bruit. Il m'a demandé si je l'avais entendu. . . .

MARCEAUX: Yes he did. One evening he had a rumbling in his bowels. He asked me did I hear that. . . .

NOLIN: J'ai répondu oui et il m'a dit, "Ça, c'était l'Esprit de Dieu. . . ."

MARCEAUX: I said yes, and he said, "That was the Spirit of God. . . ."

NOLIN: "Qui communiquait avec moi par l'intermédiaire de mon foie."

MARCEAUX: "Communicating with me through my liver."

NOLIN: Il disait que Dieu lui parlait par l'intermédiaire de toutes les parties de son corps.

MARCEAUX: He said God spoke to him through every part of his body.

DEFENCE: You mentioned a book the prisoner had written and which he showed you. . . .

MARCEAUX: Vous avez fait allusion à un livre que le prisonnier avait écrit et qu'il vous avait montré . . . .

DEFENCE: Did you notice anything unusual or extraordinary about the book?

MARCEAUX: Avez-vous rien remarqué d'inhabituel ou d'extraordinaire dans ce livre?

NOLIN: Non. Mais Riel disait qu'il l'avait écrit avec du sang de bison.

MARCEAUX: No. But Riel said it was written with buffalo blood.

DEFENCE: With buffalo blood?

MARCEAUX: Du sang de bison?

NOLIN: C'est ce qu'il a dit.

MARCEAUX: That's what he said.

DEFENCE: Did he tell you what he intended to do with the Northwest when he was in control?

MARCEAUX: Vous a-t-il dit ce qu'il comptait faire du Nord-Ouest quand il en aurait la maîtrise?

NOLIN: Il disait qu'il le diviserait et qu'il en donnerait des morceaux à diverses nationalités européennes. . . .

MARCEAUX: He said he would divide it and give portions to various European nationalities. . . .

NOLIN: Immigrants. Il disait qu'il allait donner l'Ontario à l'Irlande et qu'il allait laisser aux Ontariens le soin de s'occuper de leurs orangistes.

MARCEAUX: Immigrants. He said he would give Ontario to Ireland and let *them* worry about their Orangemen themselves.

(*Laughter in court. Suppressed.* RIEL *can control himself no longer. He gets excitedly to his feet.*)

RIEL: Your Honour, would you permit me. . . .

JUDGE (*Surprised*): Eh? What?

RIEL: I have some questions. . . .

JUDGE: No, no. At the proper time.

RIEL: Now. Now.

JUDGE: You will be given every opportunity.

RIEL: Is there any legal way I could be allowed to speak now?

JUDGE: To speak!

RIEL: To ask some questions.

JUDGE: You should suggest any questions to your counsel.

RIEL (*Urgent*): Do you allow me to speak?

JUDGE: Oh, look here, look here. . . .

RIEL: My life is at stake. I have some observations. (*Flourishes notes he's been taking.*) Some questions to ask this witness.

DEFENCE (*Suppressing indignation*): Your Honour, I don't think this is the proper time.

RIEL: Before this man leaves the witness box. . . .

JUDGE: I agree it is not the proper time. (RIEL *reluctantly sits down.*)

DEFENCE: I think it necessary the prisoner should thoroughly understand. Anything done in his behalf in this case must be done through his counsel.

JUDGE: The statute of High Treason states that a prisoner can defend himself personally. . . .

DEFENCE: Or by Counsel. But when Counsel has once been accepted. . . . (RIEL *is on his feet again.*)

RIEL: Your Honour, this case comes to be extraordinary. The Crown are trying to show that I am guilty. It is their duty. My Counsel, my good friends and lawyers whom I respect, are trying to show I am insane. It is their line of defence. I reject it. I indignantly deny that I am insane.

DEFENCE (*Trying to break in*): Your Honour. . . .

RIEL (*Not giving way*): I am not insane! I declare that in rousing and leading my people against cynical disregard and neglect by Ottawa. . . .

JUDGE: Stop! You must stop!

RIEL: The chance to ask important questions of this witness is slipping by. My good Counsel does not know this man. Counsel is not from this part of the country and does not understand our ways, and so. . . .

JUDGE: I have said you must stop. Stop! Obey!

RIEL: I will obey the Court. But I repeat my life and honour are at stake. If this man. . . .

JUDGE (*Peremptory*): Stop at once! (RIEL *sits down.*)

CROWN (*Rising. Bland. Smiling and soothing*): Your Honour, the prosecution does not object to the prisoner putting questions to the witness.

DEFENCE: We do, your Honour. The prisoner is obstructing the proper management of his case and he must not. I submit he not be allowed to interfere. . . .

JUDGE: Isn't that a matter between yourself and your client?

DEFENCE: I don't presume to argue with the court. But if we are to continue the case the prisoner must be made to abandon his attitude.

RIEL (*Rising again*): I cannot abandon my dignity. Here I have to defend myself against the accusation of high treason, or allow the plea that I am insane and consent to the animal life of an asylum. I don't care much about animal life in or out of an asylum, if it does not carry with it the moral existence of an intellectual being in full and sane possession of his faculties.

JUDGE: Stop now! No more! Stop!

RIEL (*Beaten. Despairing. Sits down*): Yes, your Honour.

CROWN: I think, your Honour, that will be the last witness for the Crown. (NOLIN *returns to his place with other witnesses.* DEFENCE *takes over.*)

DEFENCE (Lemieux): For the defence I call Father Alexis André. (ANDRÉ *takes the stand and is sworn.*) What is your name in religion?

ANDRÉ: Alexis André, Oblat.

DEFENCE: You are the Superior of the Oblats in the district of . . .?

ANDRÉ: Carlton.

DEFENCE: Since when?

ANDRÉ: For seven years. (*André speaks with a marked French accent.*)

DEFENCE: In July of '84 was there an agitation going on?

ANDRÉ: Yes. The half-breeds were demanding their rights from the federal government.

DEFENCE: What were they demanding?

ANDRÉ: Patents for their lands. Frontage on the river. Abolition of taxes on wood and timber.

DEFENCE: In what manner were these demands put forward?

ANDRÉ: The people, they sent to the government petitions, many petitions, resolutions.

DEFENCE: Any reply from the government?

ANDRÉ: I think once, yes. But only once.

DEFENCE: And that once—was it a favourable answer?

ANDRÉ: It was not favourable. Only to—put off. Your petition, it will be "taken into consideration."

DEFENCE: Up to that time, had the agitation been constitutional?

ANDRÉ: Yes. I took part in it myself.

DEFENCE: And after that time?

ANDRÉ: The silence of the government, it produced great —trouble—dissatisfaction in the people. The people, they said, "It is no good. Only if we fight." For this they send to Montana, to Riel, to come and help them.

DEFENCE: The continued neglect and evasion by the government compelled . . . . (*He is interrupted by* CROWN.)

CROWN (Osler): I object to this class of question. My learned friend has opened a case of high treason with insanity of the prisoner as his defence. Now he is trying to justify armed rebellion for the redress of grievances.

JUDGE: Which is like trying the government. Objection sustained.

DEFENCE: After Riel's arrival from Montana did the government's attitude change?

ANDRÉ: Yes. They agreed that some demands would be granted. It was not enough.

DEFENCE: Did you see Riel at Batoche?

ANDRÉ: Many times.

DEFENCE: Did he speak to you on the subjects of politics and religion?

ANDRÉ: He spoke always of politics and religion. I did not welcome this.

DEFENCE: Why?

ANDRÉ: On these subjects he had not his intelligence of mind. On other subjects he spoke with much sense. It was like he was not one man but two. Two men in him. On politics and religion he—he blew up. He was a wild man. A fool.

DEFENCE: A fool?

ANDRÉ: At least twenty times I tell him, on these subjects he is a fool. I would tell the Court something. The life of that man affected us. He was a Catholic. Very faithful. He attends to all his duties. Religious duties. But for us—the priests—he is a great anxiety. He stated many things that frightened us. We met together once—the priests—all the priests. We have to say if he can continue in his religious duties. We had to say—in politics and religion—there is no way to explain his conduct, except to say he is a fool. Insane.

DEFENCE: Insane?

ANDRÉ: Insane. (DEFENCE *gives place to* CROWN.)

CROWN (Casgrain): You say the prisoner made statements that frightened the priests. What statements?

ANDRÉ: He stated he would drive the priests from the altar, and *he* would give the sacraments himself. He would change—everything. The Mass, the liturgy. The—ceremonies and symbols. He said only the first person in the Trinity was God. He would not admit the doctrine of the Divine Presence. God was not present in the Host, according to him. He stated he would move the Vatican from Rome—to here—to North America. He demanded many reforms.

CROWN: Do you deny that a man may be a great reformer even of religious questions without being a fool?

ANDRÉ: I do not deny history.

CROWN: Is it not a fact that the half-breeds are extremely religious, and that religion has a great influence on them?

ANDRÉ: Yes. It was because Riel was so religious he had much influence on them.

CROWN: He was at pains to appear devout to the half-breeds?

ANDRÉ: I did not say "he was at pains."

CROWN: But you do say he appeared devout to the half-breeds.

ANDRÉ: Yes.

CROWN: Would you agree that he may have put religion on? Used it for a purpose?

ANDRÉ: I have said—where religion is concerned—I believe the prisoner is not of sound mind. (CROWN *gives place to* DEFENCE. ANDRÉ *returns to his seat.*)

DEFENCE (Fitzpatrick): Philippe Garnot. (GARNOT *is sworn.*) Where do you live?

GARNOT: When I am at home?

DEFENCE: Yes.

GARNOT: When I am at home I live in Batoche.

DEFENCE: Where do you live now?

GARNOT: In jail.

DEFENCE: You know the prisoner?

GARNOT: I do. Sometimes he slept at my house.

DEFENCE: Did he say anything to you about the Holy Ghost or the Spirit of God?

GARNOT: He told me the spirit of Elias was in him. He said he could prophesy. He also told me he was representing St. Peter.

DEFENCE: You say he slept at your house. On those occasions did you notice anything remarkable about his behaviour?

GARNOT: The praying. All night he was praying aloud. He kept us awake.

DEFENCE: What were the prayers?

GARNOT: They were out of his own head. He was making them up. He would say the prayer "Our Father. . . ." But the rest—I never heard them before.

DEFENCE: What did you think of that behaviour?

GARNOT: I thought the man was crazy. He acted very foolish.

DEFENCE: Would you describe him as a smooth-tempered man?

GARNOT: I would not. Sometimes he was. But if anyone contradicted him, it was like Father André said, he blew up. He had to have his own way in everything. (DEFENCE *gives place to* CROWN.)

CROWN (Robinson): The prisoner had great influence on the half-breeds, had he not?

GARNOT: He could do what he liked with them.

CROWN: You were one of his followers?

GARNOT: Against my will.

CROWN: You mean you were forced to follow him?

GARNOT: Not forced, exactly. But he came to my house with armed men. I saw it was no use resisting.

Riel • 41

CROWN: Thank you. (GARNOT *returns to his place.* CROWN *gives place to* DEFENCE.)

DEFENCE (Lemieux): Vital Fourmond. (FOURMOND *is sworn.*) What is your profession?

FOURMOND: I am a priest of St. Laurent, District of Carlton. An Oblat father.

DEFENCE: Were you present at the meeting of all the fathers when Riel was found to be insane? Insane where politics or religion are concerned.

FOURMOND: I was the one who called the meeting. (FOURMOND *speaks with a French accent.*)

DEFENCE: Were you of the same opinion as the other fathers, that on politics and religion Riel was insane?

FOURMOND: Yes.

DEFENCE: What led you to arrive at that opinion?

FOURMOND: Before the rebellion the prisoner was—he was full of laughter. Polite. Charitable. The other Riel. I agree with Father André there seemed to be two men in him. In the rebellion—once it started—he was the bad Riel. Irritable. Violent. Especially when contradicted. Once in his rage he even threatened me. He said he would burn the churches. Destroy the churches. He was—Lucifer. Lucifer. But it is also true the rage would leave him. Then—the good Riel. Then, suddenly, he is so kind. Polite. Full of apologies. Even he abases himself. This is Riel.

DEFENCE: Can you tell us more?

FOURMOND: There was much—embarrassment. He came to a meeting of the priests and he says to us, the priests, he says, "I have been appointed your spiritual adviser." Him! Riel! Our bishop! Ach!

DEFENCE: What was the priests' response to that?

FOURMOND: We told him there was one way only to make us accept that—by shooting us. We told him then he could do what he liked with our corpses. This is why we think he is insane.

DEFENCE: We have heard evidence of the prisoner's extraordinary views on doctrines of the Church and Church practices and ceremonies. Do you know of any other unusual views of his?

FOURMOND: He wanted to change the names of the days. The days of the week. He wanted to change them from pagan names to Christian names. Also, he would overthrow the Pope. He planned a tour through Canada. The States. France and Italy. In Italy he said he would overthrow His Holiness. He would choose a new Pope in Canada! A new Vatican too, he would have—in Canada! (*Laughter in court. Suppressed.*)

DEFENCE: Have you heard of a book in which he is said to have written his prophecies?

FOURMOND: Yes. It is said to be written in buffalo blood. I have not seen this book. It would be strange, to be written in buffalo blood. But, you see, this was Riel! (DEFENCE *gives place to* CROWN.)

CROWN (Casgrain): Did the prisoner make you take an oath of neutrality to his provisional government?

FOURMOND: No, no oath. There was a written promise.

CROWN: You were a close friend of the prisoner's, weren't you?

FOURMOND: At first, yes. But when I knew him better—no. The friendship ceased. Altogether.

CROWN: You have said the only way to explain Riel's conduct is to say he was insane. You would rather call him insane than say he is a criminal?

FOURMOND: I think insanity is the charitable and Christian explanation, and the right one. (CROWN *releases the witness, who goes back to his place.* DEFENCE *replaces* CROWN.)

DEFENCE (Fitzpatrick): Dr. François Roy. (ROY *is sworn.*)

You are a doctor of medicine?

ROY: Yes.

DEFENCE: In the City of Quebec?

ROY: Yes. For a great many years I have been the medical superintendent, and one of the proprietors, of the lunatic asylum at Beaufort.

DEFENCE: You have made a special study of the diseases of the brain?

ROY: Yes. (ROY *speaks with a French accent.*)

DEFENCE: You were superintendent of the asylum of Beaufort in 1875 and 1876?

ROY: Yes.

DEFENCE: In those years did you see the prisoner?

ROY: Many times.

DEFENCE: Where?

ROY: In the asylum.

DEFENCE: As a patient?

ROY: Yes.

DEFENCE: Was he admitted with all the formalities required by law?

ROY: Yes.

DEFENCE: Did you study the mental disease with which the prisoner was afflicted?

ROY: Yes—megalomania.

DEFENCE: What are the symptoms?

ROY: The patient has delusions. Grandiose delusions.

DEFENCE: That he is powerful?

ROY: Yes.

DEFENCE: A great soldier?

ROY: Yes.

DEFENCE: A great leader and statesman?

ROY: Yes.

DEFENCE: That he is identified with some biblical or other character?

ROY: Yes.

DEFENCE: That he is a great prophet, with a mission divinely inspired?

ROY: He may be a great anything and everything.

DEFENCE: Do you know of any attempt by the prisoner to identify himself with any heroic biblical character?

ROY: Yes, David. He sometimes signed his letters "Louis David Riel."

DEFENCE: Did he consider himself a prophet?

ROY: That was his constant delusion.

DEFENCE: In a case of this kind, could a casual observer, without medical experience, form an accurate estimate of the state of a man's mind?

ROY: Not usually.

DEFENCE: You were present at the examination of witnesses here today.

ROY: I was.

DEFENCE: You heard their evidence as to the prisoner's views on religion?

ROY: I did.

DEFENCE: From what you heard can you say whether, when holding and stating those views, the prisoner was of sound mind?

ROY: I believe he was of unsound mind.

DEFENCE: Do you believe he was capable or incapable of knowing the nature and quality of the acts which he committed?

ROY: I believe he was incapable.

DEFENCE: Will you swear that the man did not know what he was doing, or whether he was contrary to law in reference to his particular delusion?

ROY: That is my belief. And I positively swear it. (DEFENCE *gives place to* CROWN.)

CROWN (Osler): Under what name was the prisoner

admitted to your asylum?

ROY: Under the name of Larochelle.

CROWN: Did you know that the man was Riel?

ROY: He himself told me so.

CROWN: How many patients do you accommodate in this asylum of which you are part proprietor?

ROY: I do not know if you have a right to ask such a question.

CROWN (*Sharply*): How many patients?

ROY: About 800 or 900.

CROWN: You say you are an expert in mental diseases. Are you also an expert boarding-house keeper? (ROY, *offended, remains silent.*)

CROWN: Well? Are you?

ROY (*With dignity*): This is offensive. But I will answer. That part is for my associate proprietors. I am concerned only with the mental health of my patients.

CROWN: From what facts in evidence do you judge that the prisoner was incapable of distinguishing between right and wrong?

ROY: They never could persuade him that his special mission didn't exist.

CROWN: How would you describe his belief in his special mission?

ROY: As an insane delusion.

CROWN: Do you say that any man claiming to be inspired is suffering from an insane delusion, so as not to be able to distinguish between right and wrong?

ROY: It is possible.

CROWN: Does not the whole evidence sustain the theory that the prisoner's claim to a special mission was a skilful fraud?

ROY: There is no evidence of fraud.

CROWN: Do you say the evidence is inconsistent with fraud?

ROY (*Hesitant, puzzled*): When the prisoner was under my care. . . .

CROWN (*Irritably*): Will you answer my question . . . (*deliberately provocative*) or have you not the capacity to understand . . . ?

ROY (*Snapping back*): That may be your opinion, but. . . . (DEFENCE *intervenes coldly.*)

DEFENCE: The witness has been speaking in English. If he has difficulty in understanding the question he should ask to have it in French.

ROY (*To* CROWN): Parlez-moi en français.

JUDGE: Interpreter, please.

CROWN (*As* MARCEAUX *is on his way to the witness stand*): If he wishes to hide under the French. . . .

DEFENCE: The Act of '80 provides for the use of both languages.

JUDGE: He has the right. (*To* CROWN) What is your question?

CROWN: Do you say the evidence is inconsistent with fraud?

MARCEAUX: Diriez-vous que le témoignage est incompatible avec la fraude?

ROY: Il ne me permettait pas de répondre à cette question à ma manière auparavant. . . .

MARCEAUX: He would not let me answer that question in my own way before. . . .

ROY: Demandez-lui de reformuler la question.

MARCEAUX: Ask him to put the question another way.

CROWN (*Angry, frustrated*): If you cannot or will not answer my question in English *or* in French, I may as well let you go. You may go.

ROY (*With resentful emphasis*): Merci! (ROY, *without waiting for* MARCEAUX *to interpret* CROWN, *goes back to his place with the other witnesses, gesticulating and muttering indignantly.*

CROWN *gives place to* DEFENCE.)

DEFENCE (Fitzpatrick): Dr. Daniel Clarke. (CLARKE *is sworn.*) You come from Toronto?

CLARKE: I do.

DEFENCE: What is your position there?

CLARKE: Superintendent of the Toronto Lunatic Asylum.

DEFENCE: Have you examined the prisoner?

CLARKE: Three times.

DEFENCE: You have heard the evidence of other witnesses here?

CLARKE: I have.

DEFENCE: From your own examination and the evidence you have heard, have you formed an opinion as to the sanity or insanity of the prisoner's mind?

CLARKE (*Hesitates*): Well—assuming that the witnesses told the truth and that the prisoner at the bar was not a malingerer—there is no conclusion but that the man is certainly of unsound mind. (DEFENCE *gives place to* CROWN.)

CROWN (Osler): Are not all the facts in evidence compatible with skilful shamming by a malingerer?

CLARKE: Perhaps so.

CROWN: Do you think he is a malingerer?

CLARKE: To form an opinion on that, I should have to have him under observation day by day for months.

CROWN: Ah! But you saw Riel only yesterday and this morning! So you cannot say with certainty that he is not a malingerer? Practising fraud?

CLARKE: No, I cannot.

CROWN: Can you say whether, in what he said and did, he was able to distinguish between right and wrong?

CLARKE: I think he was. Subject to his delusions. But mind you, many of the insane know right from wrong.

CROWN: So if he knew right from wrong he was responsible for his acts?

CLARKE: That is for the Court to decide. (CROWN *gives place to* DEFENCE.)

DEFENCE (Fitzpatrick): You say the prisoner is capable of distinguishing right from wrong, subject to his delusions?

CLARKE: Yes.

DEFENCE: It has been shown that he suffered from delusions.

CLARKE: Yes. And when subject to them, he suffered to the point of insanity.

DEFENCE: Insanity?

CLARKE: Insanity.

DEFENCE (Lemieux): That closes our case in defence, your Honour. (CLARKE *to his place.* DEFENCE *gives place to* CROWN.)

CROWN (Robinson): We have some witnesses in rebuttal.

CROWN (Osler): Dr. James Wallace. (WALLACE *is sworn.*) What is your position?

WALLACE: Medical Superintendent of the Asylum for the Insane at Hamilton, Ontario.

CROWN: Have you been listening to the evidence in this case?

WALLACE: Yes.

CROWN: Have you examined the prisoner?

WALLACE: Yes.

CROWN: Have you formed an opinion as to his sanity or insanity?

WALLACE: I have not discovered any insanity about him. No indication of insanity.

CROWN: What do you say, then: is he of sound mind or not?

WALLACE: I think he is of sound mind. (CROWN *gives place to* DEFENCE.)

DEFENCE (Fitzpatrick): For how long had you the prisoner under examination?

WALLACE: Half-an-hour, alone.

DEFENCE: Really, doctor—from half-an-hour's examination you have no doubt whatever that the prisoner is of sound mind?

WALLACE: I should qualify that. I have only had that limited examination, and it does sometimes take a very long time to make sure. But from what I saw of the prisoner I found no symptoms of insanity. (WALLACE *to his place.* DEFENCE *gives way to* CROWN.)

CROWN (Robinson): Dr. Jukes. (JUKES *is sworn.*) You are a medical officer?

JUKES: I am the senior surgeon of the mounted police.

CROWN: You know the prisoner?

JUKES: I have seen him every day during his detention here.

CROWN: Have you formed an opinion as to his sanity or insanity?

JUKES: I have seen nothing to lead me to suppose he is insane. (CROWN *gives place to* DEFENCE.)

DEFENCE (Fitzpatrick): If it can be shown that a man is suffering under an insane delusion, is he responsible for any acts that he may commit while under the influence of that delusion?

JUKES: Not responsible, I should say, if it can be clearly shown that he is acting under the insane delusion.

DEFENCE: Did you hear Dr. Roy's opinion that the prisoner's belief in his special mission is an insane delusion?

JUKES: I did.

DEFENCE: If it can be proved that a man is suffering under an insane delusion that he is in communication with the Holy Ghost, and was acting under direct inspiration of God, and was bound to do a certain act and did it—would he be responsible for that act?

JUKES: Views on that subject are so different, even among

the sane. Many men have held very remarkable views on religion and have always been declared to be insane— until they gathered great numbers of followers in a new sect. Then they have become great prophets and great men. Take Mahomet, for instance. . . .

DEFENCE (*Seizing it*): Ah! So you think the conduct of Mr. Riel comparable to the conduct of Mahomet?

JUKES (*Carefully*): My opinion of Mr. Riel is rather that he is a man of great shrewdness and depth. And that he *might* have assumed, for the purpose of maintaining his influence over his followers, more than he really believed.

DEFENCE: Are you in a position to say, doctor, on your oath, that the man is not insane?

JUKES: I have never spoken to him on a single subject on which he has spoken irrationally. (JUKES *to his place again.* DEFENCE *gives way to* CROWN.)

CROWN (Robinson): General Middleton. (MIDDLETON *returns to the stand.*)

CROWN: General Middleton, you have been examined already in this case. I recall you to ask: during all your intercourse with the prisoner, did you see anything whatever to indicate unsoundness of mind?

MIDDLETON: On the contrary. I should say he was a man of rather acute intellect. He was well able to hold his own on any topic we touched on. (CROWN *gives place to* DEFENCE.)

DEFENCE (Greenshields): Did you ever hear anyone describe Mr. Riel as mad?

MIDDLETON: Oh yes. That seemed to be a pretty general opinion. One man I remember, he shrugged his shoulders and told me. "Oh!" he said. "Riel! Riel is mad. He is a fool."

DEFENCE: In your talks with the prisoner did he speak of his military operations and plans?

MIDDLETON: He seemed to have a vague idea of taking everybody prisoner—Major Crozier and myself included. Taking hostages, in fact. His idea was to exact better terms from the government.

DEFENCE: Was that a sound or feasible military idea?

MIDDLETON: Not at all. Preposterous idea. Mad, in fact. Quite mad.

DEFENCE: He spoke to you on religious subjects?

MIDDLETON: I had nothing against some of his ideas on religion. For instance, his idea that religion should be based on morality and humanity and charity. And that God's mercy was too great to be sinned away by anybody in the short time he had to live. Also he thought Rome was all wrong and that the priests were narrow-minded and interfered too much with the people. And others of his ideas were excessively good.

DEFENCE: Were certain letters sent to you by Riel?

MIDDLETON: Yes. They are among the exhibits here.

DEFENCE: Were any of them signed in an unusual or peculiar manner?

MIDDLETON: The signature was sometimes Louis Riel, sometimes Louis David Riel. I understood he included David to identify himself with the boy who slew the giant with a sling-shot.

JUDGE: Was this told you by Riel himself?

MIDDLETON: No, your Honour.

DEFENCE: Any other peculiarity in the signature?

MIDDLETON: The word exovede.

DEFENCE: Exovede?

MIDDLETON: It appeared after his name. He told me he invented it. From the Latin words *ex*, from and *ovile*, flock. From the flock. He said he used it to show he was assuming no authority except as one of the flock. An ordinary member of society. He said his Council, being composed of exovedes, was to be called exovedate.

DEFENCE (*With careful point*): And in all this, you see no indication whatever of mental abberation?

MIDDLETON: I am with those who think he put it all on— for a purpose. (MIDDLETON *to his place with the other witnesses.* DEFENCE *gives way to* CROWN.)

CROWN (Burbidge): Corporal Joseph Pigott. (PIGOTT *is sworn.*) You are a member of the North West Mounted Police?

PIGOTT: Yes, sir.

CROWN: You have had charge of the prisoner.

PIGOTT: Yes.

CROWN: You have seen him daily?

PIGOTT: I have.

CROWN: And talked with him?

PIGOTT: No, sir. No talk with him.

CROWN: But you have had frequent opportunity of observing him?

PIGOTT: Yes.

CROWN: Have you seen anything to indicate he is not of sound mind?

PIGOTT: No, sir. I always considered him to be of sound mind.

CROWN: You have heard him speak?

PIGOTT: Often, sir.

CROWN: Did he speak with good reason?

PIGOTT: With reason and politeness, sir.

CROWN: Always?

PIGOTT: Always. (PIGOTT *is released and returns to the other witnesses.*)

CROWN (Osler): Your Honour, that is the end of the evidence in reply. (*The Court is addressed by* DEFENCE.)

DEFENCE (Fitzpatrick): Your Honours, Gentlemen of the Jury. It may be well if I state at once that in defence of the prisoner we do not seek to justify him in what he did. We do not seek to justify rebellion. At the same time it is right for me to say that the government of Canada failed, wholly failed in its duty to the people here—the half-breeds, the Indians, the white settlers of these North West Territories. It is also right for me to ask, if there had been no rebellion, no shedding of blood, can any one of you honestly say that the evils under which this country suffered would have been put to rights? How is it that in the course of history what is just and right is rarely done because it is just and right, but only because force has compelled it—force, the brutal violence of war, the shedding of blood? That has been the story here. It was revealed in evidence that in the course of many years the people of these parts strove by lawful, constitutional means to obtain redress for their grievances, to secure their rights from Ottawa. With no success. But constitutional agitation in Ontario is a different matter. The Government pays attention. Not so here, two thousand miles from Ottawa. For fifteen years, gentlemen, fifteen years—the Métis could not get a single representative to lay their views before the Parliament in Ottawa. Constitutional means! When, at the urgent request of the despairing people, the accused left his place of safety in Montana—left it and came to help them, he too at first tried to wring justice from Ottawa by constitutional means. He tried. He failed. Lawful constitutional means achieved nothing. Then and not till then did the prisoner do what men of spirit have always done when goaded past endurance by gross neglect and oppression. He took up arms. He marshalled his forces, his pitifully meagre forces. Armed them. And turned to fight. David indeed—with his sling-shot against that Goliath! It was in this extremity, under the stress of this desperate resort to force, that his besetting malady, his madness, overcame his reason and took possession of his mind. Courageous it was. Heroic even. Four or five hundred flint-locks, in the hands of untrained simple men. To face the formidable might of Canada with England at her back. Courageous? Yes. Heroic? Yes. But surely also mad. This was lunacy. You have heard the evidence we have adduced of the prisoner's other lunacies. Lunatic acts. Lunatic notions and ideas. On politics. Religion. His mania. His megalomania. Even that $35,000 —the so-called bribe—his plan to use the money to start a newspaper, to rally foreign help to fight the Métis' cause —even that had its lunatic aspect. Then, that insane delusion of a mission. A special prophetic mission laid on him by God. A delusion that compelled his action and deprived him of responsibility for what he did.

Here, I confess, I tread on dangerous ground. For the prisoner is either the lunatic we have tried to make him appear or he is sane, entirely sane, in full possession of his faculties and hence responsible for everything he said and did.

There is one other consideration of which I should remind you. You are a jury of only six, none of you of the prisoner's race or religion. Which is not trial by jury as understood elsewhere. Thus the privilege of trial by the humane laws of England is denied this man.

Nevertheless, British principles of justice are safe in the hands of British jurors, here as everywhere. I know, gentlemen, that you will do this man justice. That he shall not be sent to the gallows by you, to hang high in the face of the world, a poor confirmed lunatic, a victim of oppression and injustice. (DEFENCE *returns to his seat*.)
JUDGE: Prisoner, have you any remarks to make to the jury? If so, now is your time to speak. (DEFENCE *at once interposes*.)

DEFENCE (Lemieux): May it please your Honours, earlier in the trial we though it better in the prisoner's interest that we should object to his intervention. We still do. At this stage he is entitled to make any statement he likes to the jury. But I must declare before the court that we, his counsel, must not be considered responsible for any declaration he may make.

JUDGE: Certainly. But he is entitled, and I am bound to tell him so. (*Nods to prisoner.*)

RIEL: Your Honours, Gentlemen of the Jury. (*He bows gravely to the Court.*) It would be easy for me today to play insanity. Because the circumstances are such as to excite any man. And the natural excitement my trial causes me would justify me to appear with my mind out of its ordinary condition. If I cannot speak English very well, still I will try, because most of you here speak English. I hope with the help of God I will maintain calmness and decorum, as suits this honourable Court, this honourable jury.

You have seen by the papers in the hands of the Crown that I am naturally inclined to think of God at the beginning of my actions. I wish if I do you will not take it as part of a play of insanity. (*To the wonder and embarrassment of the Court,* RIEL *clasps his hands, closes his eyes and prays, with deep humility and simplicity.*)

Oh my God, help me through thy grace and the divine influence of Jesus Christ. Oh my God, bless me. Bless this honourable Court. Bless the honourable jury. Bless my good lawyers who have come seven hundred leagues to try to save my life. Bless also the lawyers for the Crown. They have done what they thought their duty. Because they have shown fairness to me, which at first I did not expect. Oh my God, bless all who are around me, through the grace and influence of Jesus

Christ our Saviour. Change the curiosity of those who are watching me. Change that curiosity into sympathy for me. Amen. (*He opens his eyes and looks around, then begins to speak in an intimate, tender voice.*)

On the day of my birth I was helpless, and my mother took care of me, and I lived. Today, although I am a man, I am as helpless before this Court in the Dominion of Canada, and in this world, as I was helpless on the knees of my mother on the day of my birth.

The Northwest also is my mother. It is my mother country. And I am sure my mother country will not kill me . . . any more than my mother did, forty years ago when I came into this world. Because, even if I have my faults, she is my mother and will see that I am true, and be full of love for me.

When I came into the Northwest in July, the 1st of July 1884, I found the Indians suffering. I found the half-breeds eating the rotten pork of the Hudson's Bay Company. They were getting sick and weak every day. I also saw the whites. Although I am a half-breed, the greater part of my heart and blood is white. So I wanted to help also the whites to the best of my ability. I worked for them here, as I worked for them in Manitoba fifteen years ago. I can say that by the grace of God I am the founder of Manitoba. I worked to get free institutions for Manitoba. I was exiled for my pains. But today in Manitoba they have those institutions and I—I am here, hounded, outlawed, on trial for my life, forgotten in Manitoba as if I were dead.

But I am not dead. Not yet. When the glorious General Middleton fired shells and bullets thick as mosquitoes on a hot summer day, I knew that only the grace of God saved me. I said, "Oh my God I offer you all I am. All my existence I offer you to save my people. Please to make my

weakness an instrument to help my people, my country."
In hope and humility I prayed that prayer. And my
prayer was heard.

And I was given a mission. I say humbly that God—
who is in this box with me—made me his prophet.
Prophet of the New World. God directed me to lead my
people. I have led them. For months I tried to bring the
people of Saskatchewan to understand. To understand the
hand of God directing them, how best to go about getting
their grievances attended to without resort to arms. And
they were with me. We tried appeals. Petitions. Petitions
were sent to the federal government in Ottawa. Petitions
had been sent for years. But so irresponsible was that
government they hardly even bothered to reply. Instead,
instead of dealing with the just claims of the people, all
they have done is send police and more police. No answer
but police. This is insanity complicated by paralysis. I was
leading my people against this insanity when I was
attacked by armed police. I answered with arms. That is
what is called my crime of high treason, for which they
hold me today and for which they would tear me in
pieces.

If you accept the plea of the defence that I am not
responsible for my acts, then acquit me. If you pronounce
in favour of the Crown, which contends that I am responsible, acquit me all the same. You are perfectly
justified in deciding that I acted with sound mind in
quarrelling with an insane and irresponsible government.
If there is high treason, it is not mine but theirs—their
high treason against the people of the Northwest.

I am glad the Crown has proved that I am the leader of
the half-breeds. That is important to remember. It means
I stand in this dock not as myself only, but as the chosen
representative and leader of a whole people—the half-

breed people. (*Pauses impressively.*) Can a whole people be guilty of treason? (*Pauses again.*) I beg you to think of that. I am their leader—and one day perhaps I will be acknowledged as more than a leader of the half-breeds—as a leader of all that is good in this great country.

All my life I have worked for practical results. If I have succeeded, after my death my children will shake hands with the Protestants. I do not want the evils that exist in Europe to be repeated here. There will at last be a new world. But not in some days or years. It may take hundreds of years.

Yet, now, we make a beginning. We invite to our new world Italians, Poles, Bavarians, Belgians, the Swedes, the Irish, the Jews—all, all are welcome here, provided only that they will work with us and acknowledge Jesus Christ as the only hope and Saviour of the world.

Now in the soil of this great land they have their start to make a nation. Who starts the nations? God. God is the maker of the universe. Our planet is in his hands. All the nations are members of his family. To each as a good father he gives their inheritance. But God cannot create a tribe, a nation, without giving it a place. We are not birds. We have to walk on the ground. (*With passion.*) And this is our ground, our country. We will enrich it. We will cultivate it. (*Pauses.*) This is the genius of civilization.

Honourable Court, that is what I have to say. Of this I am guilty. Of the charge against me I am not guilty. I am confident that for this I will not be destroyed. (RIEL *sits down, bent over, leaning his face in his hands.* CROWN *addresses the court.*)

CROWN (Robinson): Your Honours, Gentlemen of the Jury (*deliberately in a low key*). You have been asked to believe that the man to whom you have been listening is insane. That he is incapable of knowing the nature and meaning of his acts, so as not to be able to distinguish right from wrong. Can you believe that? I submit that on the contrary he is not only sane but a man of strong and calculating mind. A man who laid his plans shrewdly. This man is not insane. He knew well enough that armed rebellion means the sacrifice of innocent lives. That it means the loss of fathers, brothers, sisters, parents, the destruction of homes. The lifelong desolation of human hearts. These are the terrible consequences of rebellion.

And yet the prisoner is a rebel. If any man deserved the scaffold, he does.

As we watch and listen to the prisoner, what do we see? In the changing light in his dark Indian eye, in his theories, religious and political, in his speaking, for he is an orator, and in French a very powerful one—we see the civilized man in him struggling with the Indian. We see the cunning, the greed, the superstition, the cruelty of the one. And the ideas and large political conceptions of the other. The egoism of Riel is excessive. His bump of self-esteem enormous. But the social bump is small. The savage in him at some point strangled the civilized man. And he was sane, gentlemen, at the time of the rebellion he was perfectly sane in the eyes of the law. That is, he was sane enough to know what he was doing, to take responsibility for his acts. And he is sane now. If he were set free he would stir up rebellion again. He would bring the same trouble on the country unless one-seventh of the North-west was handed over to him and his half-breeds and Indians. Oh, his schemes are not the work of an insane man. They are the work of misguided reasoning, reasoning based on the premise that the whole country here belongs to the Indians.

No. No, no. The plea of insanity will not bear examination. If such men as Riel were to be regarded as insane, we should need a mad-house large as half the world to confine them. But I repeat he is not insane; and if you find him guilty of the charge against him, he must suffer the penalty—the penalty with which for five centuries the law has punished the crime of high treason. (CROWN *retires.* JUDGE *charges the* JURY.)

JUDGE: Gentlemen of the Jury. It is my duty to lay down the law. It is yours to determine whether the overt acts with which the prisoner stands charged were, in fact, committed; and if so how far he participated in them. You heard the evidence. If the prisoner was implicated in these acts of war you are bound to find him guilty. If not, acquit him.

The consideration of insanity is a serious one. The law directs me to tell you that any man is presumed to be sane who is possessed of sufficient reason to be responsible for his acts. Was the prisoner so possessed? Until the contrary is proved to your satisfaction, you cannot acquit him. Did he commit those acts imputed to him while of unsound mind? If he did, did he nonetheless know he was doing wrong? Everything turns on what you decide about this.

In making your decision you, as jurymen, must not think of the prisoner alone. You must think also of the people. Their homes. The community at large who look to you for protection. You are not deciding between the government at Ottawa and the prisoner, but between the prisoner and the people of Canada. It is for you to say whether he is guilty or not guilty.

That is all I think I need say to you.

You will now retire to consider your verdict.

(*The* JURY, *accompanied by the* SHERIFF *and* CONSTABLE, *retires. The Justices then rise. Everyone in the courtroom stands while they go out. Then people begin talking.* RIEL *drops to his knees in the dock and prays. A hush falls on the crowd. Everyone turns and stares at the prisoner. For a moment his prayer can be heard.*)

RIEL: Oh my Father, help me! Help me now! According to the views of thy Providence which are beautiful and without measure. (*The people look at each other. They shake their heads. Some are moved, others cynical. Conversation is resumed.* RIEL *continues praying fervently. From time to time his words are audible.*)

(*Two reporters notice* RIEL. *Look at each other. Shrug. Their glances seem to say, "There he goes. An act. Putting on an act!" But they shake their heads. Grimace. They can't be sure. They go back to their notes.*)

(RIEL *has produced a small statuette of St. Joseph, patron saint of the Métis. His mumbled praying is heard intermittently—the Litany of St. Joseph.*)

RIEL: You promised me, St. Joseph. Help me. Do not fail me. Pray for me. Oh cover me now, St. Joseph. Cover me. Hide me.

(CROWN *is heard speaking to* DEFENCE):

CROWN: Must congratulate you. A most skilful defence.

DEFENCE: Thank you. But the jury was with you.

CROWN: Not so sure. They seemed concerned for him. Genuinely concerned. They showed a lot of sympathy for him.

(JUKES *and* CLARKE *are heard, with* ROY):

JUKES: They'll hang him, doctor!

RIEL: Lord have mercy on, us.
Christ, hear us.
Christ, graciously hear us.
God the Father in heaven, have mercy on us.
God the Son, redeemer of the world, have mercy on us.
God the Holy Ghost, have mercy on us.
Holy Trinity One God, have mercy on us.
Holy Mary, pray for us.

CLARKE: I'm not so sure.

ROY: We do not agree about him. The jury— they may not.

(MIDDLETON *and* MRS. MIDDLETON *and* MISS OSLER):

MIDDLETON: What's he up to now? Might have spared us this. Embarassing, I call it. Bit too far. Going a bit too far.

(WILLOUGHBY *and* ANDRÉ):

WILLOUGHBY: I guess he genuinely believes his saints will save him.

ANDRÉ: He has much faith.

WILLOUGHBY: Court of law —hardly the best place for miracles, Father.

(CONSTABLE *returns to court and whispers to* CLERK, *who calls Court to order.*)
CLERK: Order! Order! (*Silence falls in the courtroom. As before*, RIEL *stands. Justices enter, preceded by* SHERIFF. *Justices sit down. Court sits. Preceded by* CONSTABLE, JURYMEN *return to their box.*)

CLERK: Gentlemen of the Jury, are you agreed on your verdict?

FOREMAN (*Rising*): We are.

CLERK: How say you? Is the prisoner guilty or not guilty?

FOREMAN: Guilty.

CLERK: Look to your verdict as the Court records it: You find the prisoner Louis Riel guilty—so say you all?

FOREMAN: We do. (*To the bench*) Your Honours, there is something more.

JUDGE: What is it?

FOREMAN: I have been asked by my fellow jurors to recommend the prisoner to the mercy of the Crown.

JUDGE: Your recommendation will be forwarded in the proper manner to the proper authorities. (FOREMAN *sits down*.) Thank you, gentlemen. You may now consider yourselves discharged.

CROWN (Robinson): Will your Honour pass judgment now? I believe the proper course is to ask sentence of the Court upon the prisoner. We pray judgment.

JUDGE: Louis Riel. (RIEL *rises and bows deeply*.)

JUDGE: Have you anything to say why the sentence of the Court should not be passed upon you for the offence of which you have been found guilty?

RIEL: Yes, your Honour.

DEFENCE (Fitzpatrick): Your Honours, the Defence wishes to reserve any recourse the law may allow us hereafter.

JUDGE: Noted.

RIEL: Can I speak now?

JUDGE (*Putting up with it*): Oh yes.

RIEL: Your Honours, Gentlemen of the Jury.

JUDGE: There is no jury now. They have been discharged.

RIEL: Well, I consider them still here yet. Now that I have been condemned, it is proved at least that I am not a fool. I am not insane. If I am executed, I shall not be executed as an insane man. That will be a consolation, for my mother, my wife, my children. And for my country, my people. I think the verdict will prove that I am indeed a prophet. People will say, "He is a prophet, Riel. He suffered much. Enough to be a prophet." (*Pause. He is visibly affected.*)

JUDGE (*Wearily*): Is that all?

RIEL: If you have the kindness to permit me.

JUDGE: Well, if you must, you must.

RIEL: I have only one plea to make. My wife and family. They are without means. Father André has given a sack of flour. For my work as leader I have never had any pay. Whatever you do to me, I hope you will do something to console those who have partaken only of my sufferings. It will be rendered back to you a hundred times in this world and in the next. All that remains for me is to put myself under the protection of God my Saviour. He will not fail me. If I have been astray, I have been acting not as an impostor but according to my conscience. Your Honours, that is what I have to say.

JUDGE: Louis Riel, you have been found guilty of the most pernicious crime a man can commit. You have been found guilty of high treason. For what you did your remarks form no excuse whatever, and the law requires you to answer for it. It's true the jury has asked that your case be given merciful consideration. But I can hold out no hope that the hand of clemency will be opened to you. As for me, I have only one more duty to perform. That is, to tell you what the sentence of the law is upon you. All I can suggest or advise is that you prepare to meet your end. (RIEL *clasps his hands before his breast, bracing himself.* JUDGE *puts on the black cap.*) It is now my painful duty to pass sentence upon you. And that is, that you be taken to the police guardroom where you were last incarcerated, and that you be kept there till the 18th of September next. And that you then be taken to the place appointed for your execution, and there be hanged by the neck until you are dead. And may God have mercy on your soul. (*For a moment* RIEL *stands stricken, motionless. Then he takes the little St. Joseph, looks at it, clasps it to him.*)

RIEL (*In a low, pleading voice*): St. Joseph! (*The* CONSTABLE *takes* RIEL's *arm and leads him out. Everyone rises as the Justices leave the bench. The* CLERK, *Counsel and other officials of the Court gather up their papers. Slowly the Witnesses,* JURYMEN, REPORTERS *and spectators prepare to leave.*)